THE PALACE MUSEUM

故　宫

FOREIGN LANGUAGES PRESS　BEIJING
外文出版社　北京

THE PALACE MUSEUM

The Palace Museum, also known as the Forbidden City, is located in the heart of Being. It was the former imperial palace of the Ming (1368-1644) and Qing (1644-1911) dynasties, and is China's largest and most complete existing group of imperial palace buildings. The palace was completed in 1420 during the reign of Emperor Yongle of the Ming Dynasty.

The Forbidden City is rectangular, enclosed by a 10-meter-high battlemented wall, which extends 960 meters from north to south and 750 meters from east to west. At each of the four corners of the wall is a watchtower, and outside the wall is a moat. The Forbidden City covers an area of 720,000 square meters and contains more than 9,000 rooms. The layout of the palaces highlights the supremacy of the imperial power. The main buildings on the central axis are prominent, while the other buildings were built in strict symmetry on either side and their styles vary. The gorgeous colors, elaborate decorations and elegant furniture embody the style of typical Chinese palaces-characterized by dignity, solemnity, magnificence and orderliness.

The palace grounds are divided into two main sections, the Outer Court and the Inner Court. The Outer Court includes the Three Great Halls on the central axis—Taihedian (Hall of Supreme Harmony), Zhonghedian (Hall of

Central Harmony) and Baohedian (Hall of Preserved Harmony). On the left and right sides respectively are Wenhuadian (Hall of Literary Glory) and Wuyingdian (Hall of Martial Valor). Here the Ming and Qing emperors handled court affairs, held audiences with their officials and performed grand ceremonies. Since these palaces served as the center of the emperor's rule over the country, they were built as magnificent and stately structures. The Inner Court was where the emperors lived and dealt with daily imperial household affairs. The major buildings are Qianqinggong (Palace of Celestial Purity), Jiaotaidian (Hall of Celestial and Terrestrial Union) and Kunninggong (Palace of Terrestrial Tranquillity), commonly known as the three rear palaces. On the eastern and western sides of these major buildings are palaces and halls where the emperor's concubines and the princes and princesses lived. Other buildings, such as the Yangxindian (Hall of Mental Cultivation), and Yuhuayuan (Imperial Garden), are also located in the Inner Court.

  The Forbidden City is now called the Palace Museum, and may be regarded as China's largest museum. It has a collection of over one million works of art produced throughout China's history and household articles used in the Ming and Qing palaces. Exhibitions are regularly arranged of items kept in the museum, such as handicrafts, gold and jade, clocks and watches, bronze wares, pottery and porcelain items, and paintings. These exhibitions provide visitors with opportunities to have a taste of the imperial treasures while touring the Palace Museum.

故 宫

  故宫,旧称紫禁城,位于北京的中心,是明(1368—1644)清(1644—1911)两代的皇宫,是中国现存规模最大、最完整的帝王宫阙,建成于明朝永乐十八年(1420),至今已有近580年的历史。

  紫禁城是一座长方形的城池。南北长960米,东西宽750米,四周围有高10米的宽厚城墙。城的四隅各有一座结构精巧的角楼,城外有护城河环绕。紫禁城总面积72万平方米,拥有房屋9千余间。其建筑布局按照皇权至上的原则,保持中心突出、严格对称的形式。中轴线上的主体建筑气魄宏伟,周围环以变化的庭院,构成各异的封闭空间。局部以华丽的色彩,精致的装饰,典雅的陈设,充分体现了中国宫殿建筑庄严、肃整、华美的典型风格。

  紫禁城由外朝与内廷两大部分组成。外朝,是明清两代皇帝办理政务,举行朝会和典礼的场所,以坐落在紫禁城中轴线上的太和殿、中和殿、保和殿三大殿为中心,文华殿、武英殿为两翼,亦包括一些附属办事机构。这些宫殿是封建统治机构的中心,形制壮丽,庄严华美。内廷,是皇帝处理日常事务和生活的地方,也称后寝。内廷以乾清宫、交泰殿、坤宁宫为主体;分布在两侧的东西六宫为嫔妃的居所,乾东五所与乾西五所是皇太子们的居舍。此外还包括养心殿、御花园等建筑。与高大轩敞的外朝相比,内廷宫殿较小,布局紧凑,建筑精致,更适于起居之用。

  紫禁城如今更名为故宫博物院,它堪称是中国最大的博物馆。馆内珍藏着历代艺术品和明清宫廷文物达百万余件,内设珍宝、钟表、青铜器、陶瓷、绘画等藏品陈列馆,使人们在游访名胜古迹之余,有机会一睹传世精品的风采。

故宫导游图
Sketch Tourist Map of the Palace Museum

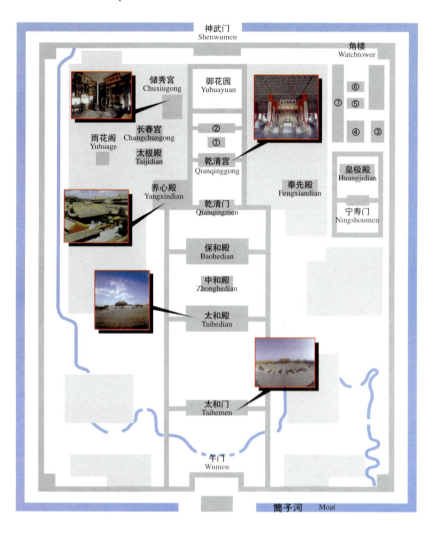

① 交泰殿 Jiaotaidian
② 坤宁宫 Kunninggong
③ 畅音阁 Changyinge
④ 养性殿 Yangxingdian
⑤ 乐寿堂 Leshoutang
⑥ 颐和轩 Yihexuan
⑦ 乾隆花园 Qianlong Garden

Buildings of the Palace Museum
The Palace Museum is the largest and most complete group of imperial palaces in China. It is divided into two sections: the Outer Court and the Inner Court. The Outer Court has three major buildings—the Taihedian, Zhonghedian and Baohedian, where the emperors dealt with state affairs, and held audiences and grand ceremonies. The Inner Court also has three major buildings—the Qianqinggong, Jiaotaidian and Kunninggong, where the emperors lived and handled day-to-day affairs.

故宫宫殿
故宫是中国现存规模最大、最完整的帝王宫阙,包括外朝和内廷两部分。外朝以太和、中和、保和三大殿为中心,是皇帝举行各种典礼和从事政治活动的场所;内廷以乾清宫、交泰殿、坤宁宫为主体,是皇帝处理政务和起居的地方。

The Palace Museum at Dawn
故宫晨曦

Corner Watchtower
At each of the four corners of the Forbidden City stands an exquisitely built watchtower. Surrounding the city wall is a 52-meter-wide and 6-meter-deep moat.

角楼
在紫禁城四隅,各踞一座精致的角楼,由九梁十八柱三重檐七十二脊构成,造型复杂精巧。城墙的外围,环绕着宽52米、深6米的护城河。

City Wall
The wall enclosing the Forbidden City is 3,428 meters long, nearly 10 meters high and 7.5 meters thick on average.

宫墙
紫禁城外围环绕着 3428 米长的城垣,高近 10 米,平均厚度为 7.5 米,外以砖砌,内填夯土,厚重而坚固。

Tiananmen (Gate of Heavenly Peace) ▷
Tiananmen is also called "Guomen"(gate of the state). It is 33.07 meters high, lofty and magnificent. During the Ming and Qing dynasties a rite would be performed here whenever there was a grand ceremony. Now it is a symbol of the City of Beijing.

天安门
又称"国门",通高 33.07 米,巍峨雄伟。明清两朝每遇大典都要在此举行仪式。如今它已成为北京的象征。

Wumen (Meridian Gate)
This is the southern main entrance of the Forbidden City. It once served as the "Arch of Triumph" for some of the Qing emperors.

午门
是紫禁城正门,上有崇楼5座,以游廊相连;东西各有一座阙亭,形如雁翅,俗称五凤楼。清朝每逢战争凯旋,皇帝都要亲临午门举行受俘礼。

Taihemen Square
This is the largest square in the Forbidden City, located between the Meridian Gate and the Gate of Supreme Harmony. An artificial river winds through here, known as the Golden Water Stream, spanned by five white marble bridges.

太和门广场
午门与太和门之间,是皇宫内最大的广场——太和门广场。广场上蜿蜒着一条着意修砌的名为"金水河"的河流,上面飞跨五座雕栏玉砌的石桥。

Taihemen (Gate of Supreme Harmony)
This is the main entrance of the Outer court and the loftiest palace gate in the Forbidden City. The Ming emperors held audiences here with their officials, and the early Qing emperors held audiences and banquets here.

太和门
为外朝的正门,也是紫禁城中最雄伟最高大的一座宫门。在明代,这里是皇帝御门听政的地方;清初,皇帝曾在这里受朝和赐宴。

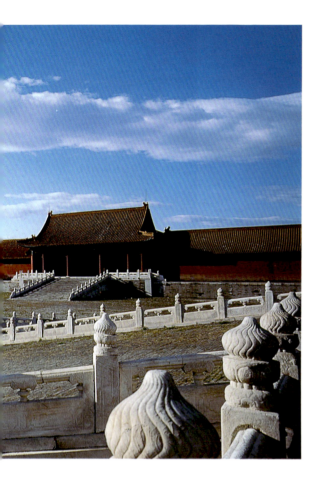

The ceiling of the Gate of Supreme Harmony is elaborately designed and beautifully decorated.

太和门内顶斗拱交错,彩画精美。

Taihedian (Hall of Supreme Harmony)
Inside Taihemen stand three main halls—
Taihedian, Zhonghedian and Baohedian.
The first to be encountered is Taihedian,
which was a symbol of the imperial power.
During the Ming and Qing dynasties important ceremonies were held here.

太和殿
进入太和门,可见在约8米高的三层台基上,矗立着三座大殿:太和殿、中和殿、保和殿。第一座大殿为太和殿,也称金銮殿,是皇权的象征。明清两代皇帝即位、大婚、册立皇后、命将出征,以及每年的重要典礼,都在这里举行。

Sundial 日晷

Bronze Crane 铜鹤

These articles were placed on the imperial terrace in front of Taihedian to symbolize the permanent stability and unity of the country.

太和殿前的丹陛上列有铜龟、铜鹤、日晷、嘉量,象征江山永固和统一。

Bronze Tortoise 铜龟

Inside the Hall of Supreme Harmony

The interior decoration of the Hall of Supreme Harmony is extravagant. The six columns inside, 13 meters high and with diameters of 1.06 meters, are gilded and carved with images of coiled dragons.

太和殿内

太和殿内装饰极尽豪华,中部矗立着6根蟠龙金漆柱,高近13米,直径达1.06米。

This is the caisson ceiling of the hall.

殿顶为金漆蟠龙吊珠藻井。

The imperial throne and the splendid carved screen behind it are placed in the middle of the back wall.

大殿正前方放置着镂空雕龙金漆御座和屏风。

Zhonghedian (Hall of Central Harmony) and Baohedian (Hall of Preserved Harmony)
Zhonghedian and Baohedian are behind Taihedian. Before a grand ceremony the emperor would rest or practice the rites in Zhonghedian. Baohedian was where he gave banquets.

中和殿与保和殿
中和殿与保和殿相继列于太和殿之后。中和殿是皇帝去太和殿参加大典前稍事休息或演习礼仪之地;保和殿是皇帝赐宴的地方。

At the back of Baohedian lies a huge carved stone with the vivid patterns of frolicking dragons amidst clouds. It is made of a single piece of stone 16 meters long, 3 meters wide and 1.7 meters thick. It weighs 250 tons, the largest of its kind in the Forbidden City.

保和殿后的云龙阶石,是宫内最大的一块石雕,由整块石头雕成。它长约16米,宽约3米,厚1.7米,重250吨。

Inside Zhonghedian
中和殿内景。

Inside Baohedian. This hall was originally a banquet hall. From the 18th century, Qing emperors began to use this hall to conduct "palace examinations"—the highest level of the imperial examination system for recruiting civil servants.

保和殿内景。这里曾为皇帝赐宴之地,18世纪后又成为清代"殿试"的固定场所。"殿试"是封建科举制度中最高一级的考试,被录取的人叫做进士,前三名称为状元、榜眼、探花。

The gargoyles in the shapes of nine animals and the phoenixriding immortal on the roof ridge of a hall are supposedly auspicious figures protecting the building.

大殿角饰。殿宇檐脊上所缀骑凤仙人及九只跑兽,有镇宅与吉祥之意。

All the roofs of the imperial buildings are paved with yellow glazed tiles, because yellow was a color reserved exclusively for the emperor.

皇帝居所皆为黄琉璃瓦顶,因在中国封建时代黄色是天子专用之色。

North of the three main halls is the Inner Court, with numerous courtyards. This was the residence of the imperial family.

位于雄伟的三大殿之北的是庭院重重的内廷,为皇室起居生活之处。

Qianqingmen (Gate of Celestial Purity)
This is the main entrance of the Inner Court. During the Qing Dynasty the emperor held audiences with his officials here. Inside Qianqingmen are the three rear palaces—Qianqinggong, Jiaotaidian and Kunninggong.

乾清门
为内廷的正门,在清代是皇帝御门听政的地方,门内有一道白石栏杆的高台通道,直达乾清宫。

These large bronze water vats were used in case of fire.
乾清门两侧排列着数口大铜缸,用来储水防备火灾。

▷

Two gilded bronze lions stand in front of Qianqingmen. They have their heads turned aside a little to face the Imperial Road, which was only used by the emperor.

乾清门前立有两座鎏金铜狮,头部微侧,皆注视皇帝御道,显示皇家的尊贵与威严。

Qianqinggong (Palace of Celestial Purity)
This palace at first served as the emperor's living quarters. Later some Inner Court ceremonies were held here. Officials were also escorted here to meet the emperor. During the Qing Dynasty the corpese of the dead emperor was laid temporarily in this palace.

乾清宫
曾为皇帝寝宫,后来成为举行内廷典礼、引见官员的地方,也是清代帝王死后停放灵柩的所在地。

Inside the Palace of Celestial Purity. High up in the middle of the hall is a plaque with an inscription which reads "Justice and Honor". Qing emperors used to hide their wills in a casket placed behind the plaque, designating their successors.

乾清宫内景。殿内正中的"正大光明"匾,曾藏过皇帝的继嗣遗诏。

Jiaotaidian (Hall of Celestial and Terrestrial Union)
This is a square hall behind the Palace of Celestial Purity, and is much smaller than the latter. During the Qing Dynasty the imperial seals were kept here. Now 25 such seals are housed in this hall.

交泰殿
位于乾清宫之后,平面呈方形,小巧玲珑,在清代是放置玉玺的地方,藏有皇帝的 25 颗印章。

Inside the Hall of Celestial and Terrestrial Union

交泰殿内景。

Gold seals used by an empress
皇后金印。

Kunninggong (Palace of Terrestrial Tranquillity)

This was the main living quarters for empresses during the Ming Dynasty. During the Qing Dynasty the emperors offered sacifices here. The Grand Nuptials of the emperor and empress were also performed here.

坤宁宫

是明朝皇后居住的正宫,清朝改为祭神的场所,也是皇帝举行大婚的地方。

Inside the main hall of the Palace of Terrestrial Tranquillity

坤宁宫正殿内景。

Dongnuange (Eastern Chamber)
This was the emperor's marital chamber in the Palace of Terrestrial Tranquillity.

坤宁宫东暖阁
这是皇帝大婚的洞房。

The emperor's bridal bed, with drapes made of red satin and embroidered with the design of 100 children, symbolizing hope for many progeny.

洞房内设龙凤喜床,床上挂有纱缦,上绣百子图,祈福皇帝子嗣昌盛。

Eastern Route
The buildings to the east of the three rear palaces are called the Eastern Route. They are Fengxiandian (Hall for Ancestral Worship), Huangjidian (Hall of Imperial Supremacy), the Theater, Yangxingdian (Studio for Cultivating Character), Leshoutang (Hall of Joyful Longevity) and Emperor Qianlong's Garden. Exhibitions of clocks and watches, handicrafts, gold and jade, and paintings are held in this area. This picture shows a narrow passageway between high, red palace walls.

东路
位于后三宫东部的宫殿群称"东路",主要包括奉先殿、皇极殿、戏台、养性殿、乐寿堂、乾隆花园等建筑。故宫藏品陈列馆如钟表馆、珍宝馆、绘画馆设在此地。图为东筒子直街,两侧高大的红墙,颇显宫院深邃。

The Clock and Watch Exhibition Hall
This was originally the Hall for Ancestral Worship, where the imperial family worshiped their ancestors. Now nearly 200 clocks and watches of various types are on permanent display here. Some of them were gifts from foreign envoys, and others were made in China, showing the excellent craftsmanship of that time.

钟表馆
原为奉先殿,是宫廷内皇家供奉先祖之处,如今辟为钟表馆,展出各式钟表近200件。故宫收藏的钟表一部分由外国使节赠送,一部分为中国自造,显示出当时高超的手工艺。

This chiming clock of Western style was made at the Qing court over 200 years ago.

清代宫廷制造的西洋自鸣钟,距今已有200多年历史。

A golden clock made during Emperor Qianlong's reign (1736-1796)

清乾隆年间(1736—1796)制的金钟。

A grandfather clock in the shape of a Chinese-style building

仿照中式建筑制造的落地钟。

This clock was presented to the Qing court by a foreign envoy.

外国使节所赠的钟表局部绘有西洋图案。

Exhibition Hall of Treasures

The Hall of Imperial Supremacy was built in imitation of the Hall of Supreme Harmony and Hall of Celestial Purity. Emperor Qianlong once manipulated state affairs from here after his alleged retirement. It is now an exhibition hall for gold and jade and other articles the imperial family used.

珍宝馆

皇极殿建筑格局仿照太和殿与乾清宫,形态气宇轩昂。原为清乾隆帝归政后的临御之殿,现辟为珍宝陈列馆,展出皇家使用的珍宝与器物。

Through the Gate of Imperial Supremacy one can see the Gate of Tranquil Longevity, which is the entrance to the magnificent Hall of Imperial Supremacy.

透过皇极门,可远远望见形制颇为雄伟的皇极殿入口——宁寿门。

A peach-shaped box plated with gold inside and a red coral shell

金胎红珊瑚壳桃式盒。

Jadeite potted landscape
翡翠盆景。

A crystal wine cup
水晶觥。

A gold buddha statuette
金佛。

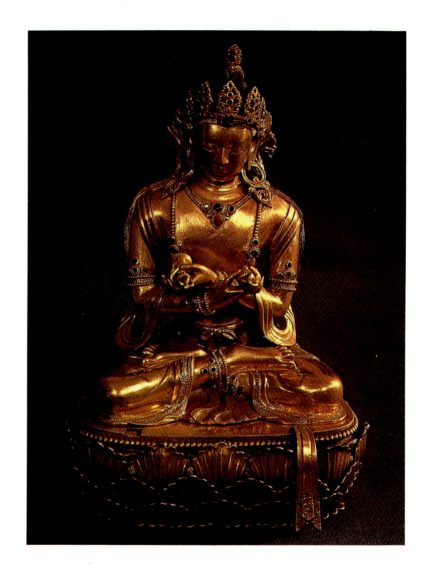

To the north of the Hall of Imperial Supremacy through the Palace of Tranquil Longevity one can see the Changyinge (Pavilion of Flowing Music) Stage and Banxilou (Theater Pavilion) in the Imperial Palace.
从皇极殿往北,穿过宁寿宫,可望见宫中的燕乐设施——畅音阁戏台与扮戏楼。

Changyinge Stage
Watching plays was the major daily recreation of the emperor, empress and concubines in the Forbidden City. The three-story Changyinge Stage is the largest theater in the Palace. The lower floors have openings in the ceilings to enable actors to move up and down freely and perform simultaneously on different floors. In this way, different scenes in Heaven and the world can be presented at the same time in a play.

畅音阁戏台
帝王嫔妃居深宫之中,日常娱乐主要是看戏。畅音阁是宫内最大的一座戏台,每逢节日及帝后的生辰、册封、登基等吉日,宫中都要演戏庆贺。戏台分上、中、下三层,层层相通,可同时演出,表现戏中天上人间的不同景象。

Leshoutang (Hall of Joyful Longevity)
This is one of a group of buildings including the Pavilion of Sustained Harmony and Pavilion of Great Auspiciousness. Emperor Qianlong once lived here after he gave up the throne to his son. Later it was used by Empress Dowager Cixi as her living quarters after she turned 60 years old.

乐寿堂
与颐和轩,景祺阁等为一组建筑群,原为清太上皇起居之所,咸丰帝(1851—1862 在位)之妃慈禧太后 60 寿辰后移居此地。

Written on the carved board is the name Leshoutang in the Chinese and Manchu languages.

乐寿堂牌匾。

Pavilion of Sustained Harmony
This beautifully built edifice is located to the north of the Hall of Joyful Longevity.

颐和轩
位于乐寿堂之北,建筑精巧华丽。

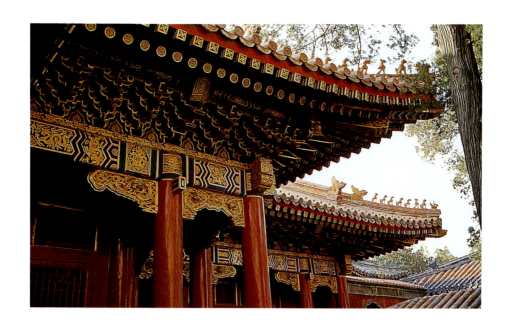

Emperor Qianlong's Garden
The garden was built during Qing Emperor Qianlong's reign (1736-1796) specially for his retirement. It resembles gardens in the region in the lower Yangtze River valley. The pavilion in the picture is called Biluoting.

乾隆花园
乾隆花园建于清朝乾隆年间,是为乾隆帝(1736—1796在位)养老休憩而设。庭院风格仿中国江南园林建筑,殿宇错落有致,间以逶迤山石和曲折游廊。图为碧螺亭。

In the Xishang Pavilion in Emperor Qianlong's Garden there is an artificial stream which winds fantastically. Wine cups were floated on it by the emperor and empress and the court officials when they amused themselves by drinking wine and composing poems here.

乾隆花园的禊赏亭内,有一个流杯渠,渠做曲状环绕。渠中放水后,可置酒杯于水上,任其漂浮。帝后大臣们常在此饮酒作诗为乐。

Western Route

The group of palaces and halls to the west of the three rear palaces is called the Western Route, including Yangxindian (Hall of Mental Cultivation) in the front and the Six Western Palaces in the rear. The Six Western Palaces include Chuxiugong (Palace for Gathering Elegance), Taijidian (Hall of the Supreme Being) and Changchungong (Palace of Eternal Spring). Pictured here is a major passageway in the Western Route.

西路

位于后三宫西面的宫殿群称"西路",前部是养心殿,后部是西六宫。西六宫包括储秀宫、太极殿、长春宫等。图为西一长街。

Yangxindian (Hall of Mental Cultivation)
Qing emperors from Emperor Yongzheng (reigned 1723-1736) lived and handled state affairs in this building.

养心殿
是清朝雍正(1723—1736 在位)以后的皇帝寝宫和处理政务之处。

The main hall of the Hall of Mental Cultivation
In the middle of the hall is a throne, on which the emperor sat when he met his officials.

养心殿正间
殿内设有宝座,是皇帝召见大臣的地方。

Sanxitang (Hall of Three Rarities)
This is a delicate structure to the west of the Hall of Mental Cultivation. Works by three leading ancient Chinese calligraphers were kept here, hence the name.

三希堂
位于养心殿西端,房间纤巧精致,因藏有著名书法家王羲之、王献之、王珣的著名法贴,得名三希堂。

The Eastern Chamber of the Hall of Mental Cultivation
Empress Dowager Cixi used to "hold court behind the curtain" here, which meant that two thrones were placed in the chamber, one in front of a yellow gauze curtain and the other behind it. The child emperor Guangxu met the officials openly while Cixi announced her decisions from behind the curtain.

养心殿东暖阁
曾为慈禧太后"垂帘听政"之处。所谓"垂帘听政",是指在室内设前后两个宝座,年幼的皇帝坐在前面,太后坐在后面召见大臣,中间隔以黄纱帘。

Portrait of Emperor Guangxu

Emperor Guangxu (reigned 1875-1908) was enthroned at the age of four, while Empress Dowager Cixi held the real power. As an adult he supported political reform of the Qing Dynasty and was imprisoned by Cixi. He died suddenly two days before Cixi herself died.

光绪皇帝像

1875—1908年在位,4岁登基,由慈禧垂帘听政。成年后支持改革,被慈禧囚禁,于慈禧去世前2天猝卒。

Yuhuage (Raining Flowers Pavilion)
This is a Lamaist building in which Buddhist statues from the western regions were enshrined. Buddhist services used to be held here for the imperial family.

雨花阁
宫中喇嘛教建筑,内供西天梵像,是清宫从事宗教活动的场所。

Taijidian (Hall of Supreme Being)
Called Weiyanggong (Palace of the Young Night) in the Ming Dynasty and Hall of Supreme Being in Qing, this was the concubines' residence.

太极殿
在明朝名为未央宫,清朝改为太极殿,是明清两代妃子的居所。

Inside the Hall of Supreme Being

太极殿内景。

◁
Changchungong (Palace of Eternal Spring)
This palace was a residence for Ming emperors' concubines. During the Qing Dynasty, Empress Dowager Cixi and concubines of the last emperor, Pu Yi (reigned 1909-1911), once lived here.

长春宫
曾是明朝皇妃的住所,慈禧太后及末代皇帝溥仪(1909—1911在位)的妃子先后居住在此。

Chuxiugong (Palace for Gathering Elegance)
This was once Empress Dowager Cixi's residence. Cixi spent 630,000 taels of silver fitting up this palace to celebrate her 50th birthday. The decorations and furniture inside the palace are extremely lavish.

储秀宫
储秀宫是慈禧太后生前居住过的地方。慈禧50大寿时,曾耗银63万两装修此宫,宫内陈设极为华丽奢侈。

The sumptuous furniture in the western chamber of the Palace for Gathering Elegance

储秀宫西里间的精美陈设。

Portrait of Empress Dowager Cixi
Cixi (1835-1908) was first a concubine of Emperor Xianfeng. After Xianfeng's death in 1861, she seized state power through a coup and was the real ruler of the country for the next 48 years.

慈禧太后像
慈禧(1835－1908)为咸丰帝之妃,在咸丰去世后通过政变,控制国家大权达48年之久。

◁
Inside the eastern chamber of the Palace for Gathering Elegance

储秀宫东间内景。

The Imperial Garden
The garden covers an area of 12,000 square meters, dotted by more than 20 towers and pavilions of various sizes. Pictured here is the Tianyi Gate.

御花园
为明朝所建,清初加以修缮,是供帝后们游赏的花园。它占地为1.2万平方米,有大小20余座殿阁,结构精巧别致,古雅富丽。图为御花园内的天一门。

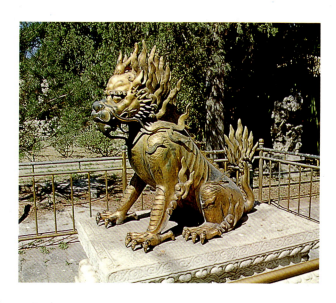

In front of the Tianyi Gate is a pair of gilded statues of *xiezhi*, a mythical beast believed to have the power to discern between right and wrong.

天一门外陈列一对鎏金铜獬豸。獬豸是中国古代传说中善辨忠奸的一种神兽。

Exotic rockery in front of the Tianyi Gate
天一门前的奇石盆景。

◁
Inside the Tianyi Gate one can see a pine and a cypress with their branches interlocked. They are called the "loving-couple" trees.

进入天一门,可见一株松树和一株柏树上端交扭一处,称为"连理树"。人们常以此树喻爱情忠贞。

Qin'andian (Hall of Imperial Peace)
This hall is in the center of the Imperial Garden, where sacrifices were offered to the Daoist God of Water.

钦安殿
钦安殿位于御花园的正中心,是祭祀道教"玄天上帝"的场所。

Wanchunting (Pavilion of Many Springs)
This is one of the twin pavilions in the Imperial Garden, the other is called Qianqiuting (Pavilion of Many Autumns).

万春亭
御花园内有两座形态近似的亭子，万春亭与千秋亭。万春亭上圆下方，形态优美。

Duixiushan (Hill of Soaring Elegance)
At the top of this artificial hill one can have a panoramic view of the Forbidden City. Every year on the seventh day of the seventh lunar month, the Mid-autumn Festival and the Double Ninth Festival, the emperor, empress and concubines would climb the hill to celebrate.

堆秀山
为人工堆就。登山远眺,紫禁城美景可尽收眼底。清宫中每逢七夕、中秋和重阳节,帝后嫔妃都要在此处登高赏玩。

Shenwumen (Gate of Divine Might)
This is the north gate of the Forbidden City. In the gate tower a bell and a drum were used to mark the passage of the hours. During the Qing Dynasty, concubine candidates were ushered in and out of the Forbidden City through this gate.

神武门
为紫禁城的北门,门楼上设有钟鼓,为宫内打更报时。清代选秀女、宫女时从此门出入。

图书在版编目(CIP)数据

故宫/曹蕾编．－北京：外文出版社，1997.5
ISBN 7-119-02071-4

Ⅰ．故… Ⅱ．曹… Ⅲ．故宫-画册 Ⅳ．K928.74-64
中国版本图书馆CIP数据核字(96)第07489号

Text by：Cao Lei
Edited by：Ying Ren
Photos by：Meng Zi　Lin Jing　Xu Yanzeng
　　　　　　Sun Shuming　Liu Chungen
　　　　　　Luo Zhewen　Tang Shaowen
　　　　　　Li Shaobai　Hu Baoyu
　　　　　　Tong Bo　Hu Weibiao
Translated by：Li Jing
Bookcover designed by：Tong Bo
Plates designed by：Tong Bo

The Palace Museum

ISBN 7-119-02071-4

© Foreign Languages Press 1997
Published by Foreign Languages Press
24 Baiwanzhuang Road，Beijing 100037，China
Printed in the People's Republic of China

编撰：曹　蕾
责任编辑：应　人
摄影：蒙　紫　林　京　许延增　孙树明
　　　刘春根　罗哲文　唐少文　李少白
　　　胡宝玉　佟　博　胡维标
翻译：李　晶
封面设计：佟　博
图版设计：佟　博

故　宫

曹蕾 编

ⓒ 外文出版社
外文出版社出版
(中国北京百万庄大街24号)
邮政编码100037
深圳当纳利旭日印刷有限公司印刷
1997年(24开)第一版
1997年第一版第一次印刷
(英汉)
ISBN 7-119-02071-4/J・1405(外)
003900 (精)